A Little Book About...

Bees

The Honey-Bee in Lore and Literature

Printed in the United Kingdom

First Edition, 2015

ISBN-13: 978-1508903994

ISBN-10: 1508903999

Contents

Seeley Jackson, 'Bees and Berries' (1875)

A Very Little History of...
Bee-Keeping

Humans and bees have had a very long relationship indeed. Depictions of humans collecting honey from wild bees date to some 15,000 years ago, and efforts to domesticate them are shown in Egyptian art around 4,500 years ago. Thus today's bee-keepers (or apiarists) are joining a very old, and venerable tradition!

Ancient apiculture (from the Latin *apis* meaning 'bee') used simple hives and smoke, with honey stored in jars. It wasn't until the eighteenth century however, that European understandings of the colonies and biology of bees allowed the construction of the 'movable comb hive' so that honey could be harvested without destroying the entire colony.

Despite its relative simplicity, in prehistoric Greece (Crete and Mycenae), there existed a system of high-status apiculture, as concluded from the finds of hives, smoking pots, honey extractors and other beekeeping paraphernalia. It was an incredibly highly valued industry, controlled by beekeeping overseers. These men wore gold rings depicting apiculture scenes; a further signifier of the esteem in which beekeeping was held - that these everyday sights replaced traditional religious imagery.

Beekeeping was by no means an isolated practice, and many other archaeological finds have been discovered. One of the most significant has been at 'Rehov' (a Bronze and Iron Age archaeological site in the Jordan Valley, Israel), where thirty intact hives, made of straw and unbaked clay, were discovered - dating from about 900 BCE. The hives were found in orderly rows, three high, in a manner that could have accommodated around 100 hives, held more than 1 million bees, and had a potential annual yield of 500kg of honey and 70kg of beeswax! As the reader will discover in the course of this book, such practices were discussed at length by some of the best Ancient Greek and Roman thinkers, including Aristotle, Aristophanes, Virgil and Varro.

Despite its long history, early examples of artificial hives (made from hollow logs, wooden boxes, pottery vessels and woven straw baskets or 'skeps'), remained relatively unchanged for the next thousand years or so. It was not until the eighteenth century that European natural philosophers undertook the scientific study of bee colonies. Jan Swammerdam and René Antoine Ferchault de Réaumur (Dutch and French scientists respectively) were among the first to use a microscope and dissection to understand the internal biology of honey bees. Réaumur was among the first to construct a glass walled observation hive to better observe activities within hives. He observed queens laying eggs in open cells, but still had no idea of how a queen was fertilized; nobody had ever witnessed the mating of a queen and drone - and many theories held that queens were 'self-fertile.'

Early forms of honey collecting entailed the destruction of the entire colony when the honey was harvested. The wild hive was crudely broken into, using smoke to suppress the bees, the honeycombs were torn out and smashed up - along with the eggs, larvae and honey they contained. The liquid honey from the destroyed brood nest was strained through a sieve or basket. This was destructive and unhygienic, but for hunter-gatherer societies this did not matter, since the honey was generally consumed immediately and there were always more wild colonies to exploit. But in settled societies the destruction of the bee colony meant the loss of a valuable resource. This drawback made beekeeping both inefficient and something of a 'stop and start' activity. There could be no continuity of production and no possibility of selective breeding, since each bee colony was destroyed at harvest time, along with its precious queen.

Intermediate stages in the transition from the 'old beekeeping' to the new were recorded by Thomas Wildman in 1768/1770, who described various advances. For example, Wildman fixed a parallel array of wooden bars across the top of a straw hive to which, as he discovered - the bees fixed their combs to. Wildman also described a further development, using hives with 'sliding frames' for the bees to build their comb, foreshadowing more modern uses of movable-comb hives. However, the forerunners of the hives that are mainly used today are considered the traditional basket top bar (movable comb) hives of Greece, known as 'Greek Beehives'. The oldest testimony on their use dates back to 1669, although it is probable that their use is more than 3000 years old. Rather appropriately, knowledge had come full circle!

The nineteenth century saw this revolution in beekeeping practices completed through the perfection of the movable comb hive by the American Lorenzo Lorraine Langstroth (1810 - 1895). Langstroth was the first person to make practical use of earlier discoveries that there was a specific spatial measurement between the wax combs, later called *the bee space*, which bees do not block with wax, but keep as a free passage. Having determined this bee space (between 5 and 8 mm), Langstroth then designed a series of wooden frames within a rectangular hive box, carefully maintaining the correct space between successive frames, and found that the bees would build parallel honeycombs in the box without bonding them to each other, or to the hive walls. The honeycombs could thus be removed and returned for filling. The invention and development of the movable-comb-hive fostered the growth of commercial honey production on a large scale in both Europe and the USA. It ushered in the popular interest in bees and honey-bees that we see today; for amateur and professional keepers alike.

Although there have been many advancements in the way we care for, and work with the honey-bee, they are facing a perilous point in their history. Climate change, pesticides and urban development have all impacted on their survival. With the continued destruction of their natural environment (largely unchanged until the last hundred years), combined with the addition of poisons to the very pollens they survive on - the future of the honey-bee is uncertain indeed. We can all do a little to help, for example by planting bee-friendly flowers or going 'pesticide-free', but for those looking to get a little more involved - take a look at some of these fantastic charities:

Greenpeace:

http://sos-bees.org/

The British Beekeeper's Association:

http://www.bbka.org.uk/

The Bumble Bee Conservation Trust:

http://bumblebeeconservation.org/

Aesop's Fables

Aesop's Fables, or the *Aesopica*, is a collection of fables credited to Aesop – a slave and storyteller believed to have lived in Ancient Greece between 620 and 560 BCE. Aesop himself is a fascinating character, and even his very existence remains uncertain. None of his actual tales have survived, though numerous tales credited to him have been gathered across the centuries, in many languages, in a storytelling tradition that continues to this day.

Apollonius of Tyana, a first century CE philosopher, is recorded as having said about Aesop:

> "Like those who dine well off the plainest dishes, he made use of humble incidents to teach great truths, and after serving up a story he adds to it the advice to do a thing or not to do it."

Like the humble bees, who dine so finely from their carefully procured honey, Aesop's tales contain great wisdom. Indeed, Aristophanes, in his comedy *The Wasps*, represented the protagonist Philocleon as having learnt the "absurdities" of Aesop from conversation at banquets, and Plato wrote in *Phaedo* that Socrates whiled away his jail time turning some of Aesop's fables "which he knew" into verses. Short, pithy and ever-resistant to an overall narrative or moralising impulse, the following lines teach us not only about bees and their hives, but also of ourselves and the communities we live in.

The Flies and the Honey-Pot

A number of Flies were attracted to a jar of
honey which had been overturned in a
housekeeper's room, and placing their feet in it,
ate greedily. Their feet, however, became so
smeared with the honey that they could not use
their wings, nor release themselves, and were
suffocated. Just as they were expiring, they
exclaimed,

*"O foolish creatures that we are, for the sake of
a little pleasure we have destroyed ourselves."*

Pleasure bought with pains, hurts.

The Bee and Jupiter
(How the Bee got her sting)

A bee from Mount Hymettus, the queen of the hive,
ascended to Olympus to present Jupiter some honey
fresh from her combs. Jupiter, delighted with the
offering of honey, promised to give whatever she
should ask. She therefore besought him, saying,

*"Give me, I pray thee, a sting, that if any mortal shall
approach to take my honey, I may kill him."*

Jupiter was much displeased, for he loved the race of
man, but could not refuse the request because of his
promise. He thus answered the Bee:

*"You shall have your request, but it will be at the peril of
your own life. For if you use your sting, it shall
remain in the wound you make, and then you will die
from the loss of it."*

Evil wishes, like chickens, come home to roost.

The Bee and the Fly

A Bee, observing a Fly frisking about her hive, asked him, in a very passionate tone, what he did there? "Is it for such scoundrels as you, said she, to intrude into the company of the queens of the air?"

"You have great reason, truly," replied the Fly, "to be out of humour. I am sure they must be mad who would have any concern with so quarrelsome a nation."

"And why so? Thou saucy malapert," returned the enraged Bee: "We have the best laws, and are governed by the best policy in the world. We feed upon the most fragrant flowers, and all our business is to make honey: honey which equals nectar, though tasteless wretch, who livest upon nothing but putrefaction and excrement."

"We live as we can", rejoined the Fly. "Poverty, I hope, is no crime; but passion is one, I am sure. The honey you make is sweet, I grant you; but your heart is all bitterness: for to be revenged on an enemy you will destroy your own life; and are so inconsiderate in your rage, as to do more mischief to yourselves than to your adversary. Take my word for it, one had better have less considerable talents, and use them with more discretion."

The greatest genius with a vindictive temper is far surpast in point of happiness by men of talents less considerable.

The Wasps and the Bees

Pretenders of very kind are best detected by appealing to their works.

Some honeycombs being claimed by a swarm of Wasps, the right owners protested against their demand, and the cause was referred to a Hornet. Witnesses being examined, they deposed that certain winged creatures, who had a loud hum, were of a yellowish colour, and somewhat like Bees, were observed a considerable time hovering about the place where this nest was found. But this did not sufficiently decide the question; for these characteristics, the Hornet observed, agreed no less with the Bees than with the Wasps. At length a sensible old Bee offered to put the matter upon this decisive issue:

"Let a place be appointed by the court", said he, "for the plaintiffs and defendants to work in. It will then soon appear which of us are capable of forming such regular cells, and afterwards of filling them with so delicious a fluid."

The Wasps refusing to agree to this proposal, sufficiently convinced the judge on which side the right lay, and he decreed the honey-combs accordingly.

It is a folly to arrogate works to ourselves of which we are by no means capable.

A Gnat and a Bee

A Gnat, half starved with cold and hunger, went one frosty morning to a Bee-hive, to beg a charity; and offered to teach music in the Bee's family, for her diet and lodging. The Bee very civilly desired to be excluded: "For", says she, "I bring up all my children to my own trade, that they may be able to get their living by their industry; and I am sure I am right; for see what music, which you would teach my children, has brought you yourself to."

Industry ought to be diligently inculcated in the minds of children of all ranks and degrees; for who stands so sure as to say he is exempt from the vicissitudes of this uncertain life?

The Wasps
Aristophanes (424 BCE)

Aristophanes (c. 446 - 386 BCE) was a comic playwright of ancient Athens. Eleven of his thirty plays survive virtually complete, and these, tougher with some fragments of his other plays, provide the only real examples of the genre of comic drama known as 'Old Comedy.' *The Wasps* was the fourth of his plays, and in it, Arisophanes pokes satirical fun at the demagogue Cleon - but also the system that gives him his power - the Athenian courts of law.

We have a master of great renown, who is now sleeping up there on the other story. He has bidden us keep guard over his father, whom he has locked in, so that he may not go out. This father has a curious complaint; not one of you could hit upon or guess it, if I did not tell you....

He is a merciless judge, never failing to draw the convicting line and return home with his nails full of wax like a bumble-bee. Fearing he might run short of pebbles he keeps enough at home to cover a sea-beach, so that he may have the means of recording his sentence. Such is his madness, and all advice is useless; he only judges the more each day.

The Oeconomicus
Xenophon (362 BCE)

The Oeconomicus is a Socratic dialogue, written by Xenophon (c. 430 - 354 BCE), principally about household management and agriculture. Beyond the emphasis on domestic economics, the dialogue deals with such topics as the qualities and relationships of men and women, rural vs. urban life, slavery, religion, and education. The extract below outlines his views on the roles of men and women in the household, using the honey-bee as his ideal paradigm. Whilst modern readers may find the gender dynamics (somewhat!) outdated, it forms a fascinating insight into the significance bees have had to past societies, relationships and culture more broadly.

Thus I addressed her, Socrates, and thus my wife made answer: "But how can I assist you? what is my ability? Nay, everything depends on you. My business, my mother told me, was to be sober-minded!"...

"To my mind they are not the things of least importance," I replied, "unless the things which the queen bee in her hive presides over are of slight importance to the bee community; for the gods. The gods, my wife, would seem to have exercised much care and judgment in compacting that twin system which goes by the name of male and female, so as to secure the greatest possible advantage to the pair. Since no doubt the underlying principle of the bond is first and foremost to perpetuate through procreation the races of living creatures; and next, as the outcome of this bond, for human beings at any rate, a provision is made by which they may have sons and daughters to support them in old age....

I added: "Just such works, if I mistake not, that same queen-bee we spoke of labours hard to perform, like yours, my wife, enjoined upon her by God Himself."

"And what sort of works are these?" she asked; "what has the queen-bee to do that she seems so like myself, or I like her in what I have to do?"

"Why," I answered, "she too stays in the hive and suffers not the other bees to idle. Those whose duty it is to work outside she sends forth to their labours; and all that each of them brings in, she notes and receives and stores against the day of need; but when the season for use has come, she distributes a just share to each. Again, it is she who presides over the fabric of choicely-woven cells within. She looks to it that warp and woof are wrought with speed and beauty. Under her guardian eye the brood of young is nursed and reared; but when the days of rearing are past and the young bees are ripe for work, she sends them out as colonists with one of the seed royal to be their leader."...

"Nay," she answered, "that will be my pleasantest of tasks, if careful nursing may touch the springs of gratitude and leave them friendlier than before."

And I was struck with admiration at her answer, and replied: "Think you, my wife, it is through some such traits of forethought seen in their mistress-leader that the hearts of bees are won, and they are so loyally affectionate towards her that, if ever she abandon her hive, not one of them will dream of being left behind; but one and all must follow her."

Thomas Bewick (1753 - 1828)
Illustration for Aesop's 'A Gnat and a Bee'

The Georgics
Virgil (29 BCE)

The Georgics (from the Greek meaning 'On Working the Earth') is an epic poem by Virgil (70 - 19 BCE); ostensibly on the everyday running of a farm, though also providing moral instruction on living 'the good life.' Virgil was a keen bee-keeper himself, and dedicates a whole section (Book III) to bees and bee keeping - continually fluctuating between intense optimism and pessimistic gloom.

Virgil is ranked as one of Rome's greatest poets, known principally for his three major works: *The Eclogues, The Georgics* and the ambitious *Aeneid* (modelled after Homer's *Iliad* and *Odyssey*). In the passage below, his intense respect for the honey-bee, its work and societal structure is evidenced...

Come, then, I will unfold the natural powers
Great Jove himself upon the bees bestowed,
The boon for which, led by the shrill sweet strains
Of the Curetes and their clashing brass,
They fed the King of heaven in Dicte's cave.

Alone of all things they receive and hold
Community of Offspring, and they house
Together in one city, and beneath
The shelter of majestic laws they live;
And they alone fixed home and country know,
And in the summer, warned of coming cold,
Make proof of toil, and for the general store
Hoard up their gathering harvesting.

For some watch o'er the victualling of the hive,
And these by settled order ply their tasks afield;
And some within the confines of their home
Plant firm the comb's first layer, Narcissus' tear,
And sticky gum oozed from the bark of trees,
Then set the clinging wax to hang therefrom.

Others the while lead forth the full-grown young,
Their country's hope, and others pres and pack
The thrice repured honey, and stretch their cells
To bursting with the clear-strained nectar sweet.
Some too, the wardship of the gates befalls,
Who watch in turn for showers and cloudy skies...

A hum arises: hark! They buzz and buzz
About the doors and threshold; till at length
Safe laid to rest they hush them for the night,
And welcome slumber laps their weary limbs...

Led by these tokens, and with such traits to guide,
Some say that unto bees a share is given
Of the Divine Intelligence, and to drink
Pure draughts of ether; for God permeates all -
Earth, and wide ocean, and the vault of heaven -
From whom flocks, herds, men, beasts of every kind,
Draw each at birth the fine essential flame;
Yea, and that all things hence to Him return,
Brought back by dissolution, nor can death
Find place: but, each into his starry rank,
Alice they soar, and mount the heights of heaven.

Aristaeus and the 'Death of the Bees'

This tale, dealing with the very origins of bees, comes from Ovid's *Fasti;* a six-book poem published in 8 CE. Aristaeus was a minor god in Greek mythology, credited with the discovery of bee-keeping. As the legend goes - Eurydice, the wife of Orpheus, died when she was bitten by a snake whist being pursued by Aristaeus. As a consequence of her death, his beloved bees died. In order to effect their resurrection he had to sacrifice an ox to her spirit - as 'one life axed bred a thousand.'

Aristaeus wept, when he saw all his bees killed and honeycombs abandoned incomplete. His sea-blue mother [the Naiad Kyrene] could scarcely console his pain, and attached these final words to her speech:

'Stop your tears, my boy. Proteus [The sea-god] will lighten your loss, and tell you how to regain what is gone. But so he does not baffle you by altering appearance, clamp his two hands in strong chains.'

The youth approaches the seer and binds the limp arms of the sleeping old man of the ocean. Proteus uses his art to shift and feign his looks, but soon resumes shape, mastered by chains. Lifting his dripping face and sea-blue beard, he said:

'You seek a technique to recover bees? Sacrifice a bullock and inter its carcass: the one interred will supply what you seek.'

The shepherd follows orders. From the putrid ox swarms bubble. One life axed bred a thousand.

The Song of Solomon
The Bridegroom praises the Bride...

Thy lips, O my spouse, drop as the honeycomb:
Honey and milk are under thy tongue;
And the smell of thy garments is like the smell of Lebanon

The Bible
(Proverbs 24:13-14)

Eat honey, my son, for it is good. Honey from the comb is sweet
to your taste.

Know also that wisdom is like honey for you: If you find it, there
is a future hope for you, and your hope will not be cut off.

The Qur'an
(Ayyats 68 and 69)

And the Lord taught the Bee to build its cells in hills, in trees,
and in men's habitats; then to eat of all the produce and find with
the skill the precious paths of its Lord: there issues from within
their bodies a drink of varying colours, wherein is healing for
men.

Verily this is a sign for those who give thought.

Saint Ambrose

Saint Ambrose (340 - 397 CE), was a bishop of Milan who became one of the most influential ecclesiastical figures of the fourth century. There is a legend that as an infant, a swarm of bees settled on his face while he lay in his cradle, leaving behind a drop of honey. His father considered this a sign of his future eloquence and honeyed tongue, and was heartened at his infant son's prospects. It is for this reason that bees and beehives often appear in the saint's symbology.

He used bees as metaphors in many of his writings - here expounding on the Song of Songs, and comparing virginity with the life of bees...

Let, then, your work be as it were a honeycomb, for virginity is fit to be compared to bees, so laborious is it, so modest, so continent. The bee feeds on dew, it knows no marriage couch, it makes honey. The virgin's dew is the divine word, for the words of God descend like the dew. The virgin's modesty is unstained nature. The virgin's produce is the fruit of the lips, without bitterness, abounding in sweetness. They work in common, and their fruit is in common.

How I wish you, my daughter, to be an imitator of these bees, whose food is flowers, whose offspring is collected and brought together by the mouth. Do imitate her, my daughter. Let no veil of deceit be spread over your words; let them have no covering of guile, that they may be pure, and full of gravity.

S. AMBROSIVS.

In Greek mythology, ambrosia (directly translating as 'of the immortals') was the food and drink of the gods, often depicted as conferring longevity or immortality upon whoever consumed it. In the modern day, it is better known as... honey! Ambrosia was very closely related to the gods' other form of sustenance, nectar, and the two terms may not have been originally distinguished. In Homer's epic poems, nectar was generally the drink, and ambrosia the food of the gods. It was with ambrosia that Athena prepared Penelope in her sleep, so that when she appeared for the final time before her suitors, the effects of the years had been stripped away – and the suitors inflamed with passion at the sight of her.

On the other hand, in Alcman (a choral lyric poet from Sparta), nectar is the food, and in Sappho (the great female lyric poet, from the island of Lesbos) and Anaxandrides (an Athenian poet), ambrosia is the drink. When a character in Aristophanes' Knights says, "I dreamed the goddess poured ambrosia over your head—out of a ladle," the homely and realistic ladle brings the ineffable honeyed-nectar back into the earthly realm – thankfully, for us mere mortals to enjoy.

The bee is more honoured
than other animals;

Not because she labours, but
because she labours for others.

- Saint John Chrysostom. Archbishop of Constantinople
(347 - 407 CE).

An Old English Nursery Rhyme

Bless you, bless you, bonny bee:
Say, when will your wedding be?
If it be tomorrow day,
Take your wings and fly away.

An Old English Saying

A swarm of bees in May is worth a load of hay
A swarm of bees in June is worth a silver spoon
A swarm of bees in July is not worth a fly!

Euphues and His England
John Lyly (1580)

- The first mention of the phrase 'as busy as a bee' in the
English language!

Travailing thus like two Pilgrimes, they thought it most
necessary to direct their steppes toward London, which
they hard was the most royall seat of the Queene of
England. But first they came to Caunterbury, an olde Citie,
somewhat decayed, yet beautiful to behold, most famous
for a Cathedrall Church, the very Majestie whereoff, stroke
them into a maze, where they saw many monuments, and
heard tell of greater, then either they ever saw, or easely
would beleeve.

After they had gone long, seeing them-selves almost
benighted, determined to make the nexte house their Inne,
and espying in their way even at hande a very pleasaunt
garden, drew neere: where they sawe a comely olde man as
busie as a Bee among his Bees, whose countenaunce
bewrayed his conditions: this auncient Father, Euphues
greeted in this manner.

William Shakespeare

Cassius:
Antony,
The posture of your blows are yet unknown;
But for your words, they rob the Hybla bees,
And leave them honeyless.

Antony:
Not stingless too.

Brutus:
O, yes, and soundless too;
For you have stol'n their buzzing, Antony,
And very wisely threat before you sting.

- Antony, Brutus and Cassius speaking on 'the plains of Philippi'
in Act V, scene i, of *Julius Caesar* (1599).

For this, be sure, to-night thou shalt have cramps,
Side-stitches that shall pen thy breath up; urchins
Shall, for that vast of night that they may work,
All exercise on thee; thou shalt be pinch'd
As thick as honeycomb, each pinch more stinging
Than bees that made 'em.

- Prospero speaking on 'the island' in Act I, scene ii, of
The Tempest (1611).

Those who have handled sciences have been either men of experiment or men of dogmas.

The men of experiment are like the ants, they only collect and use; the reasoners resemble spiders, who make cobwebs out of their own substance.

But the bee takes a middle course: it gathers its material from the flowers of the garden and of the field, but transforms and digests it by a power of its own. Not unlike this is the true business of philosophy; for it neither relies solely or chiefly on the powers of the mind, nor does it take the matter which it gathers from natural history and mechanical experiments and lay it up in the memory whole, as it finds it, but lays it up in the understanding altered and digested.

- Francis Bacon (1561 - 1626); the English philosopher, statesman and scientist - dubbed the 'father of empiricism'. His works established and popularised inductive reasoning, often called the *Baconian Method* - marking a new turn in scientific investigation. Set out in the *Novum Organum* (1620), Bacon's observations on the methods of the ants, the spiders and the bees, still hold true today.

The Fable of the Bees
Bernard Mandeville (1714)

The Fable of The Bees: or, Private Vices, Public Benefits is a book written by Bernard Mandeville (1670 - 1733). It consists of a poem, with a prose discussion of its themes, and was first published in 1714. The poem, whilst ostensibly dealing with a colony of bees, suggests many key principles of economic thought, including division of labour and the "invisible hand", seventy years before these concepts were more thoroughly elucidated by Adam Smith. As it turns out, one can learn a lot from bees!

Mandeville intended his poem as a commentary on contemporary England, setting forth "the appalling plight of a prosperous community in which all the citizens suddenly take it into their heads to abandon luxurious living, and the State to cut down armaments, in the interests of saving." At the time of its publication, the poem was considered scandalous – largely being seen as an attack on Christian virtues. Keynes noted that it was "convicted as a nuisance by the grand jury of Middlesex in 1723... standing out in the history of the moral sciences for its scandalous reputation."

A Spacious Hive well stock'd with Bees,
That lived in Luxury and Ease;
And yet as fam'd for Laws and Arms,
As yielding large and early Swarms;
Was counted the great Nursery
Of Sciences and Industry.
No Bees had better Government,
More Fickleness, or less Content.
They were not Slaves to Tyranny,
Nor ruled by wild Democracy;
But Kings, that could not wrong, because
Their Power was circumscrib'd by Laws....

Vast Numbers thronged the fruitful Hive;
Yet those vast Numbers made 'em thrive
Millions endeavouring to supply
Each other's Lust and Vanity
Whilst other Millions were employ'd,
To see their Handy-works destroy'd;
They furnish'd half the Universe;
Yet had more Work than Labourers.
Some with vast Stocks, and little Pains
Jump'd into Business of great Gains;
And some were damn'd to Sythes and Spades,
And all those hard laborious Trades
Where willing Wretches daily sweat,
And wear out Strength and Limbs to eat:
Whilst others follow'd Mysteries,
To which few Folks bind Prentices
That want no Stock, but that of Brass,
And may set up without a Cross;
As Sharpers, Parasites, Pimps, Players,
Pick-Pockets, Coiners, Quacks, Sooth-Sayers,
And all those, that, in Enmity
With down-right Working, cunningly
Convert to their own Use the Labour

Of their good-natur'd heedless Neighbour.
These were called Knaves; but, bar the Name,
The grave Industrious were the Same.
All Trades and Places knew some Cheat,
No Calling was without Deceit....

Thus every Part was full of Vice,
Yet the whole Mass a Paradice;
Flatter'd in Peace, and fear'd in Wars
They were th' Esteem of Foreigners,
And lavish of their Wealth and Lives,
The Ballance of all other Hives.
Such were the Blessings of that State;
Their Crimes conspired to make 'em Great;
And Vertue, who from Politicks
Had learn'd a Thousand cunning Tricks,
Was, by their happy Influence,
Made Friends with Vice: And ever since
The Worst of all the Multitude
Did something for the common Good.

*The 'hive' is corrupt but prosperous, yet it grumbles about
lack of virtue. A higher power decides to give them what
they ask for:*

But Jove, with Indignation moved,
At last in Anger swore, he'd rid
The bawling Hive of Fraud, and did.
The very Moment it departs,
And Honesty fills all their Hearts;
There shews 'em, like th' Instructive Tree,
Those Crimes, which they're ashamed to see;
Which now in Silence they confess,
By Blushing at their Uglyness;
Like Children, that would hide their Faults,
And by their Colour own their Thoughts;

Imag'ning, when they're look'd upon,
That Others see, what they have done.

This results in a rapid loss of prosperity, though the newly virtuous hive does not mind:

Now mind the glorious Hive, and see,
How Honesty and Trade agree:
The Shew is gone, it thins apace;
And looks with quite another Face,
For 'twas not only that they went,
By whom vast Sums were Yearly spent;
But Multitudes, that lived on them,
Were daily forc'd to do the Same.
In vain to other Trades they'd fly;
All were o'er-stock'd accordingly....

So few in the vast Hive remain;
The Hundredth part they can't maintain
Against th' Insults of numerous Foes;
Whom yet they valiantly oppose:
Till some well-fenced Retreat is found;
And here they die, or stand their Ground.
No Hireling in their Armies known;
But bravely fighting for their own,
Their Courage and Integrity
At last were crown'd with Victory.
They triumph'd not without their Cost;
For many Thousand Bees were lost.
Hard'ned with Toils, they counted Ease itself a Vice;
Which so improved their Temperance;
That, to avoid Extravagance,
They flew into a hollow Tree,
Blest with Content and Honesty.

The Moral

Then leave Complaints: Fools only strive
To make a Great an honest Hive.
T' enjoy the World's Conveniencies,
Befamed in War, yet live in Ease
Without great Vices, is a vain
Eutopia seated in the Brain.
Fraud, Luxury, and Pride must live;
Whilst we the Benefits receive.
Hunger's a dreadful Plague, no doubt,
Yet who digests or thrives without?
Do we not owe the Growth of Wine
To the dry, crooked, shabby Vine?
Which, whilst its Shutes neglected stood,
Choak'd other Plants, and ran to Wood;
But blest us with its Noble Fruit;
As soon as it was tied, and cut:
So Vice is benefcial found,
When it's by Justice lopt, and bound;
Nay, where the People would be great,
As necessary to the State,
As Hunger is to make 'em eat.
Bare Vertue can't make Nations live
In Splendour; they, that would revive
A Golden Age, must be as free,
For Acorns, as for Honesty.

Divine Songs
Isaac Watts (1715)

How doth the little busy Bee
Improve each shining Hour,
And gather Honey all the Day
From ev'ry op'ning Flow'r!

How skilfully she builds her Cell!
How neat she spreads the Wax!
And labours hard to store it well
With the sweet Food she makes.

Proverbs of Hell
William Blake (1793)

A fool sees not the same tree that a wise man sees.
He whose face gives no light, shall never become a star.
Eternity is in love with the productions of time.
The busy bee has no time for sorrow.

There was an Old Man in a tree,
Who was horribly bored by a Bee;
When they said, "Does it buzz?"
He replied, "Yes, it does!
It's a regular brute of a Bee!"

- A Book of Nonsense
Edward Lear (1846)

The Bee

Like trains of cars on tracks of plush
I hear the level bee:
A jar across the flowers goes,
Their velvet masonry

Withstands until the sweet assault
Their chivalry consumes,
While he, victorious, tilts away
To vanquish other blooms.

His feet are shod with gauze,
His helmet is of gold;
His breast, a single onyx
With chrysoprase, inlaid.

His labour is a chant,
His idleness a tune;
Oh, for a bee's experience
Of clovers and of noon!

- Emily Elizabeth Dickinson (1830 - 1836). An American
poet born in Amherst, Massachusetts, Dickinson had a
prolific output. She was a strongly introverted and reclusive
woman however, and fewer than a dozen of her nearly
1,8000 poems were published during her lifetime.

The Pedigree of Honey

The pedigree of honey
Does not concern the bee;
A clover, any time, to him
Is aristocracy.

- Emily Dickinson.

Come Down O' Maid
Alfred Lord Tennyson (1847)

So waste not thou; but come; for all the vales

Await thee; azure pillars of the hearth

Arise to thee; the children call, and I

Thy shepherd pipe, and sweet is every sound,

Sweeter thy voice, but every sound is sweet;

Myriads of rivulets hurrying thro' the lawn,

The moan of doves in immemorial elms,

And murmuring of innumerable bees.

I don't like to hear cut and dried sermons.

No - when I hear a man preach, I like to see him act as if he were fighting bees!

- Abraham Lincoln (1809 - 1865); the sixteenth president of the United States.

"Our treasure lies in the beehive of our knowledge. We are perpetually on the way thither, being by nature winged insects and honey gatherers of the mind."

- Friedrich Wilhelm Nietzsche (1844 - 1900). The quotation above appears in Nietzsche's *On the Genealogy of Morals* (1887); a polemic tracing the evolution of moral concepts. Nietzsche hoped to undermine 'moral prejudices', specifically the corrupt morality of Christianity and Judaism.

The keeping of bees is like the direction of sunbeams.

- Henry David Thoreau (1817 - 1862); an American naturalist, author, poet and philosopher, known for his reflections on simple living in natural surroundings.

Handle a book as a bee does a flower, extract its sweetness but do not damage it.

- John Muir (1838 - 1914); the Scottish-American naturalist, author, and early advocate of the preservation of wilderness in the United States.

I have not yet forgotten the first apiary I saw, where I learned to love the bees. It was many years ago, in a large village of Dutch Flanders...

Here, as in all places, the hives lent a new meaning to the flowers and the silence, the balm of the air and the rays of the sun. One seemed to have drawn very near to the festival spirit of nature. One was content to rest at this radiant crossroad, where the aerial ways converge and divide that the busy and tuneful bearers of all country perfumes unceasingly travel from dawn unto dusk. One heard the musical voice of the garden, whose loveliest hours revealed their rejoicing soul and sang of their gladness. One came hither, to the school of the bees, to be taught the preoccupations of all-powerful nature, the harmonious concord of the three kingdoms, the indefatigable organization of life, and the lesson of ardent and disinterested work; and another lesson too, with a moral as good, that the heroic workers taught there, and emphasized, as it were, with the fiery darts of the myriad wings, was to appreciate the somewhat vague savour of leisure, to enjoy the almost unspeakable delights of those immaculate days that revolved on themselves in the fields of space, forming merely a transparent globe, as void of memory as the happiness without alloy.

- *The Life of the Bee* (1901), by Maurice Maeterlinck (1862 - 1949). Maeterlinck was a Belgian playwright and poet, awarded the Nobel Prize in Literature in 1911, 'in appreciation of his many-sided literary activities.' His work largely centres around death and the meaning of life - and where better to start looking than in *The Life of a Bee!*

From *The Tacuinum Sanitatis* - a medieval handbook (written around
the fifteenth century) on health and wellbeing. It was based on
the *Taqwim al-sihha*; an eleventh-century Arab medical treatise,
penned by Ibn Butlan of Baghdad.

For just as bees know how to extract honey from flowers, which to men are agreeable only for their fragrance and colour, even so here also those who look for something more than pleasure and enjoyment in such writers may derive profit for their souls. Now, then, altogether after the manner of bees must we use these writings, for the bees do not visit all the flowers without discrimination, nor indeed do they seek to carry away entire those upon which they light, but rather, having taken so much as is adapted to their needs, they let the rest go. So we, if wise, shall take from heathen books whatever befits us and is allied to the truth, and shall pass over the rest. And just as in culling roses we avoid the thorns, from such writings as these we will gather everything useful, and guard against the noxious.

- Frederick Morgan Padelford (1875 - 1942), 'Address to Young Men on the Right Use of Greek Literature' from *Essays on the Study and Use of Poetry by Plutarch and Basil the Great* (1902).

The Queenless Hive
Leo Tolstoy, *War and Peace* (1869), 'Book XI, Chapter XX'

Meanwhile Moscow was empty. There were still people in it, perhaps a fiftieth part of its former inhabitants had remained, but it was empty. It was empty in the sense that a dying queenless hive is empty.

In a queenless hive no life is left though to a superficial glance it seems as much alive as other hives. The bees circle round a queenless hive in the hot beams of the midday sun as gaily as around the living hives; from a distance it smells of honey like the others, and bees fly in and out in the same way. But one has only to observe that hive to realize that there is no longer any life in it. The bees do not fly in the same way, the smell and the sound that meet the beekeeper are not the same. To the beekeeper's tap on the wall of the sick hive, instead of the former instant unanimous humming of tens of thousands of bees with their abdomens threateningly compressed, and producing by the rapid vibration of their wings an aerial living sound, the only reply is a disconnected buzzing from different parts of the deserted hive.

From the alighting board, instead of the former spirituous fragrant smell of honey and venom, and the warm whiffs of crowded life, comes an odour of emptiness and decay mingling with the smell of honey. There are no longer sentinels sounding the alarm with their abdomens raised, and ready to die in defence of the hive. There is no longer the measured quiet sound of throbbing activity, like the sound of boiling water, but diverse discordant sounds of disorder. In and out of the hive long black robber bees smeared with honey fly timidly and shiftily. They do not sting, but crawl away from danger. Formerly only bees laden with honey flew into the hive, and they flew out empty; now they fly out laden.

The beekeeper opens the lower part of the hive and peers in. Instead of black, glossy bees- tamed by toil, clinging to one another's legs and drawing out the wax, with a ceaseless hum of labour- that used to hang in long clusters down to the floor of the hive, drowsy shrivelled bees crawl about separately in various directions on the floor and walls of the hive. Instead of a neatly glued floor, swept by the bees with the fanning of their wings, there is a floor littered with bits of wax, excrement, dying bees scarcely moving their legs, and dead ones that have not been cleared away. The beekeeper opens the upper part of the hive and examines the super. Instead of serried rows of bees sealing up every gap in the combs and keeping the brood warm, he sees the skilful complex structures of the combs, but no longer in their former state of purity. All is neglected and foul.

Black robber bees are swiftly and stealthily prowling about the combs, and the short home bees, shrivelled and listless as if they were old, creep slowly about without trying to hinder the robbers, having lost all motive and all sense of life. Drones, bumblebees, wasps, and butterflies knock awkwardly against the walls of the hive in their flight. Here and there among the cells containing dead brood and honey an angry buzzing can sometimes be heard. Here and there a couple of bees, by force of habit and custom cleaning out the brood cells, with efforts beyond their strength laboriously drag away a dead bee or bumblebee without knowing why they do it. In another corner two old bees are languidly fighting, or cleaning themselves, or feeding one another, without themselves knowing whether they do it with friendly or hostile intent. In a third place a crowd of bees, crushing one another, attack some victim and fight and smother it, and the victim, enfeebled or killed, drops from above slowly and lightly as a feather, among the heap of corpses.

The keeper opens the two centre partitions to examine the brood cells. In place of the former close dark circles formed by thousands of bees sitting back to back and guarding the high mystery of generation, he sees hundreds of dull, listless, and sleepy shells of bees. They have almost all died unawares, sitting in the sanctuary they had guarded and which is now no more. They reek of decay and death. Only a few of them still move, rise, and feebly fly to settle on the enemy's hand, lacking the spirit to die stinging him; the rest are dead and fall as lightly as fish scales. The beekeeper closes the hive, chalks a mark on it, and when he has time tears out its contents and burns it clean.

The Swarming of the Bees
Henry Van Dyke (1909)

Who can tell the hiding of the white bees' nest?
Who can trace the guiding of their swift home flight?
Far would be his riding on a life-long quest:
Surely ere it ended would his beard grow white.

Never in the coming of the rose-red Spring,
Never in the passing of the wine-red Fall,
May you hear the humming of the white bee's wing
Murmur o'er the meadow, ere the night bells call.

Wait till winter hardens in the cold grey sky,
Wait till leaves are fallen and the brooks all freeze,
Then above the gardens where the dead flowers lie,
Swarm the merry millions of the wild white bees.

Out of the high-built airy hive,
Deep in the clouds that veil the sun,
Look how the first of the swarm arrive;
Timidly venturing, one by one,
Down through the tranquil air,
Wavering here and there,
Large, and lazy in flight,–

Caught by a lift of the breeze,
Tangled among the naked trees,–
Dropping then, without a sound,
Feather-white, feather-light,
To their rest on the ground.

Thus the swarming is begun.
Count the leaders, every one
Perfect as a perfect star
Till the slow descent is done.
Look beyond them, see how far
Down the vistas dim and grey,
Multitudes are on the way.
Now a sudden brightness
Dawns within the sombre day,
Over fields of whiteness;
And the sky is swiftly alive
With the flutter and the flight
Of the shimmering bees, that pour
From the hidden door of the hive
Till you can count no more.

Now on the branches of hemlock and pine
Thickly they settle and cluster and swing,
Bending them low; and the trellised vine
And the dark elm-boughs are traced with a line
Of beauty wherever the white bees cling.
Now they are hiding the wrecks of the flowers,
Softly, softly, covering all,
Over the grave of the summer hours
Spreading a silver pall.
Now they are building the broad roof ledge,

Into a cornice smooth and fair,
Moulding the terrace, from edge to edge,
Into the sweep of a marble stair.
Wonderful workers, swift and dumb,
Numberless myriads, still they come,
Thronging ever faster, faster, faster!
Where is their queen? Who is their master?
The gardens are faded, the fields are frore,–
How will they fare in a world so bleak?
Where is the hidden honey they seek?
What is the sweetness they toil to store
In the desolate day, where no blossoms gleam?
Forgetfulness and a dream!

But now the fretful wind awakes;
I hear him girding at the trees;
He strikes the bending boughs, and shakes
The quiet clusters of the bees
To powdery drift; He tosses them away,
He drives them like spray;
He makes them veer and shift
Around his blustering path.
In clouds blindly whirling,
In rings madly swirling,
Full of crazy wrath,
So furious and fast they fly
They blur the earth and blot the sky
In wild, white mirk.
They fill the air with frozen wings
And tiny, angry, icy stings;
They blind the eyes, and choke the breath,
They dance a maddening dance of death

Around their work,
Sweeping the cover from the hill,
Heaping the hollows deeper still,
Effacing every line and mark,
And swarming, storming in the dark
Through the long night;
Until, at dawn, the wind lies down,
Weary of fight.
The last torn cloud, with trailing gown,
Passes the open gates of light;
And the white bees are lost in flight.

Look how the landscape glitters wide and still,
Bright with a pure surprise!
The day begins with joy, and all past ill,
Buried in white oblivion, lies
Beneath the snowdrifts under crystal skies.
New hope, new love, new life, new cheer,
Flow in the sunrise beam,–
The gladness of Apollo when he sees,
Upon the bosom of the wintry year,
The honey-harvest of his wild white bees,
Forgetfulness and a dream!

"But you had retired, Holmes. We heard of you as living the life of a hermit among your bees and your books on a small farm."

Sherlock replies: "Exactly, Watson. Here is the fruit of my leisured ease, the magnum opus of my latter years... *The Practical Handbook of Bee Culture.*"

- Sir Arthur Conan Doyle (1859 - 1930), *His Last Bow* (1917). 'The Practical Handbook of Bee Culture' plays a greater part in the mystery than anyone might expect - helping Holmes to overcome his nemesis, the German spy; Von Bork.

On Pleasure

And now you ask in your heart,

"How shall we distinguish that which is good in pleasure from that which is not good?"

Go to your fields and your gardens, and you shall learn that it is the pleasure of the bee to gather honey of the flower,

But it is also the pleasure of the flower to yield its honey to the bee.

For to the bee a flower is a fountain of life,

And to the flower a bee is a messenger of love,

And to both, bee and flower, the giving and the receiving of pleasure is a need and an ecstasy.

People of Orphalese, be in your pleasures like the flowers and the bees.

- *The Prophet* (1923); a book of twenty-six prose poetry essays written by the Lebanese artist, philosopher and writer, Kahlil Gibran (1883 - 1931).

The Lake Isle of Innisfree
William Butler Yeats (1888)

I will arise and go now, and go to Innisfree,
And a small cabin build there, of clay and wattles made:
Nine bean-rows will I have there, a hive for the honey-bee,
And live alone in the bee-loud glade.

And I shall have some peace there, for peace comes
dropping slow,
Dropping from the veils of the mourning to where the
cricket sings;
There midnight's all a glimmer, and noon a purple glow,
And evening full of the linnet's wings.

I will arise and go now, for always night and day
I hear lake water lapping with low sounds by the shore;
While I stand on the roadway, or on the pavements grey,
I hear it in the deep heart's core.

Last night as I was sleeping,

I dreamt – marvellous error!

that I had a beehive

here inside my heart.

And the golden bees

were making white comb

and sweet honey

from my old failures.

- Antonio Machado (1875 - 1939), a Spanish poet and one
of the leading figures of the Spanish literary movement
known as the 'Generation of '98'.

Did you know...?

Honey-Bees are the only insect that produces food eaten by man.

Bees have 170 odorant receptors, compared with only 62 in fruit flies and 79 in mosquitoes.

The honey bee's wings stroke incredibly fast, about 200 beats per second, or 12,000 beats per minute. This makes their famous and distinctive buzz.

A honey bee can fly for up to six miles, and as fast as 15 miles per hour.

A honey bee visits 50 to 100 flowers during a collection trip. Foraging bees have to fly about 55,000 miles to produce a pound of honey, visiting around 2 million flowers.

A hive of bees will fly 90,000 miles - the equivalent of three orbits around the earth to collect 1 kg of honey.

The average worker bee produces about 1/12th of a teaspoon of honey in her lifetime.

A colony of bees consists of 20,000-60,000 honeybees and one queen. Worker honey bees are female, live for about six weeks, and do all the work.

In the summer (when the hive needs to be at its maximum strength) a Queen bee can lay up to 2,500 eggs a day. She can control whether she lays male or female eggs.

Once honey bee eggs hatch into worker larvae, they'll be fed around 1,300 times per day!

It is estimated that 1100 honey bee stings are required to be fatal.

www.ingramcontent.com/pod-product-compliance
Lightning Source LLC
Chambersburg PA
CBHW050513290526
45786CB00007B/2550